Thank you for your recent purchase. We hope you love it! If you do, would you consider posting an online review? This helps us to continue providing great products and helps potential buyers to make confident decisions. Thank you in advance for your review and for being a preferred customer.

This Book Belongs To

HOW TO DRAW BEAR

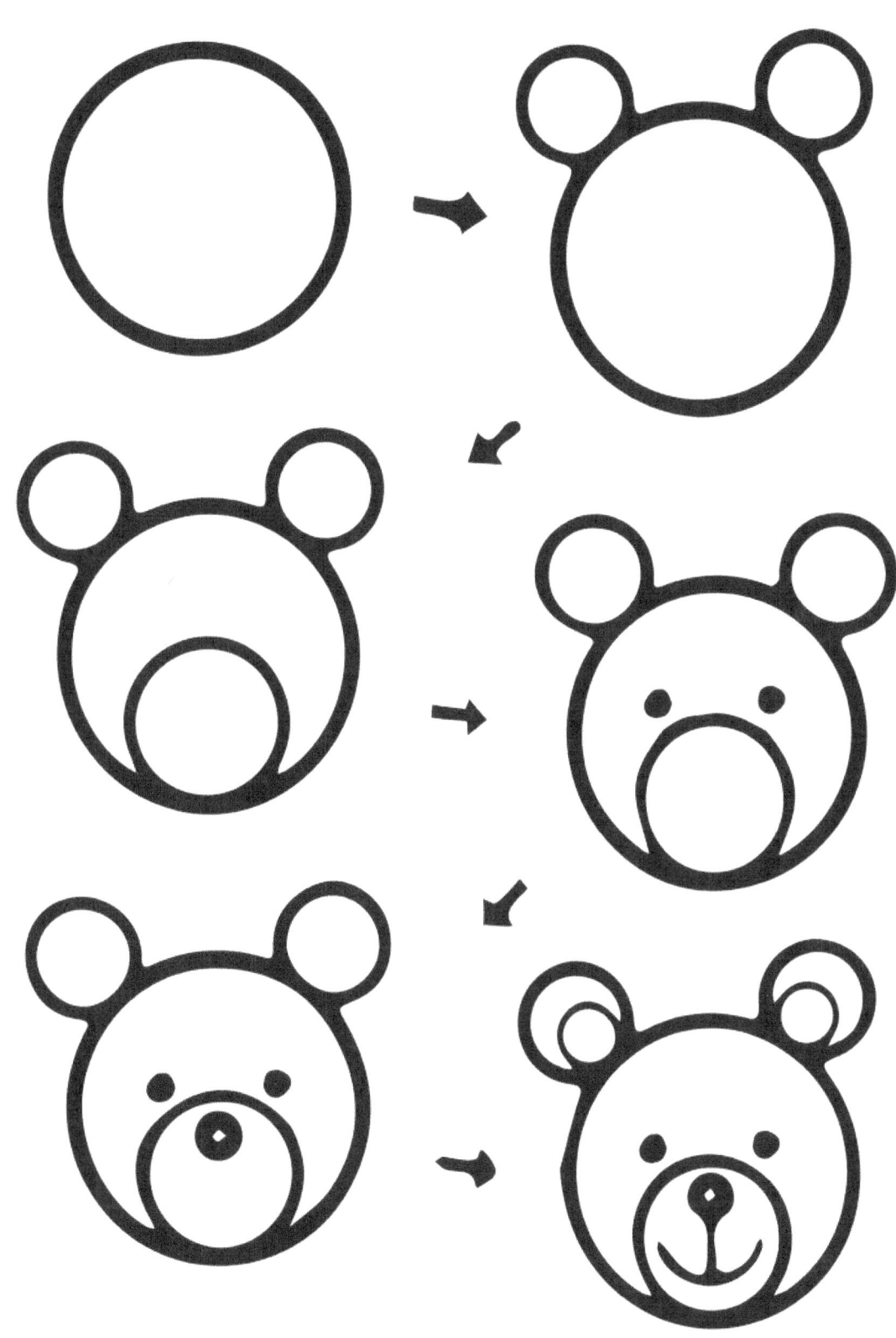

Draw Yourself

HOW TO DRAW BOY

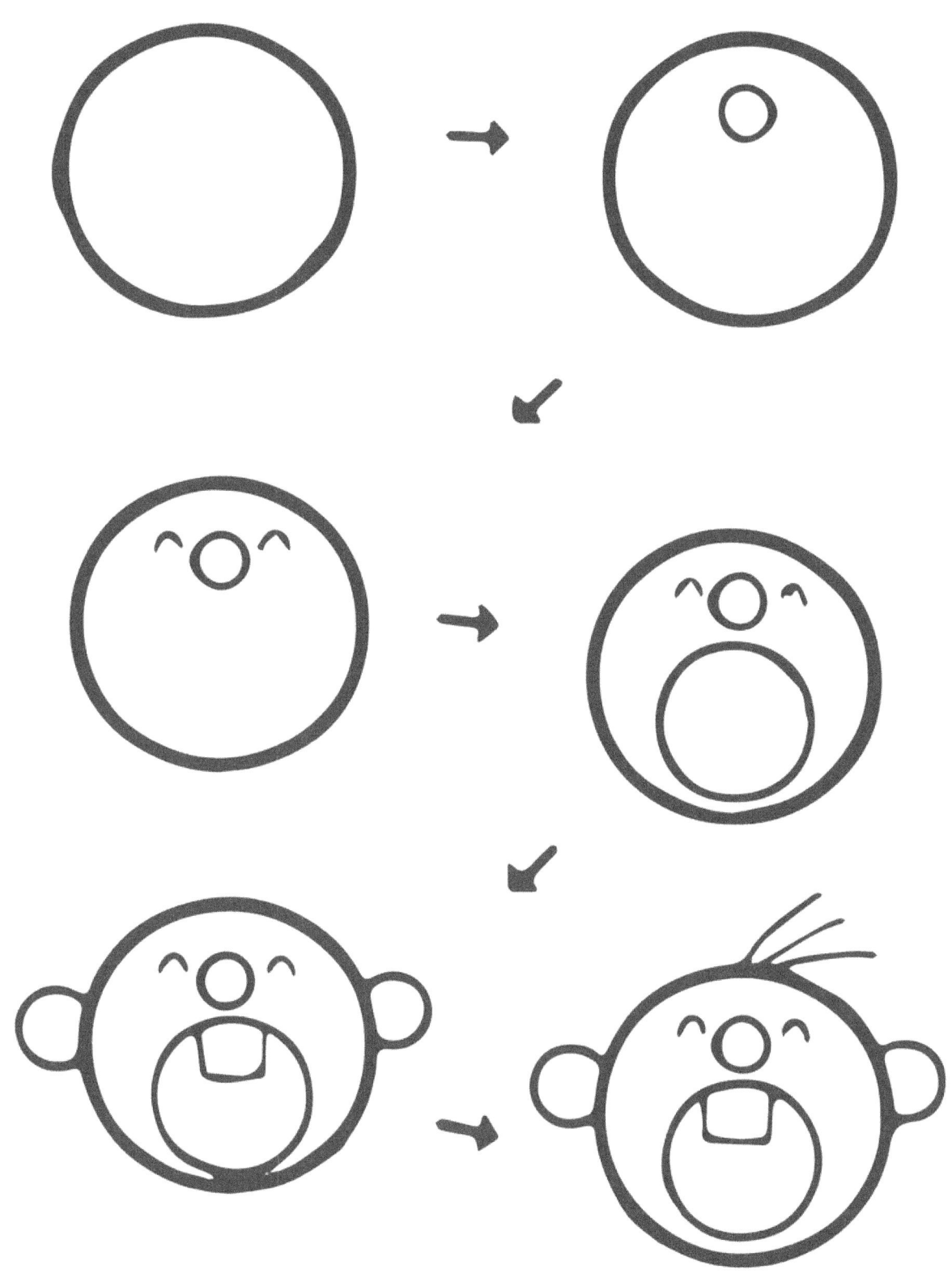

Draw Yourself

HOW TO DRAW BULL

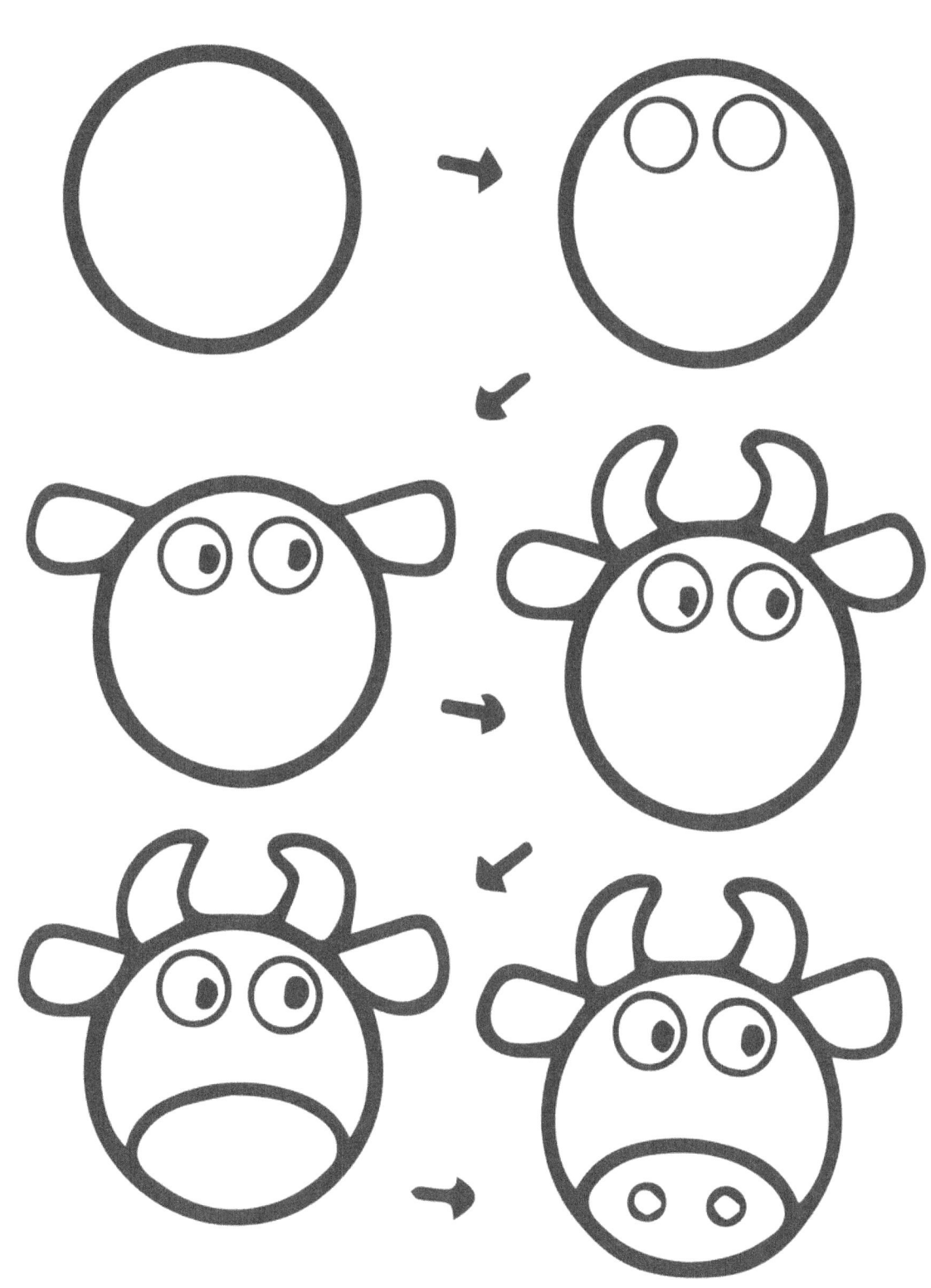

Draw Yourself

HOW TO DRAW BULL

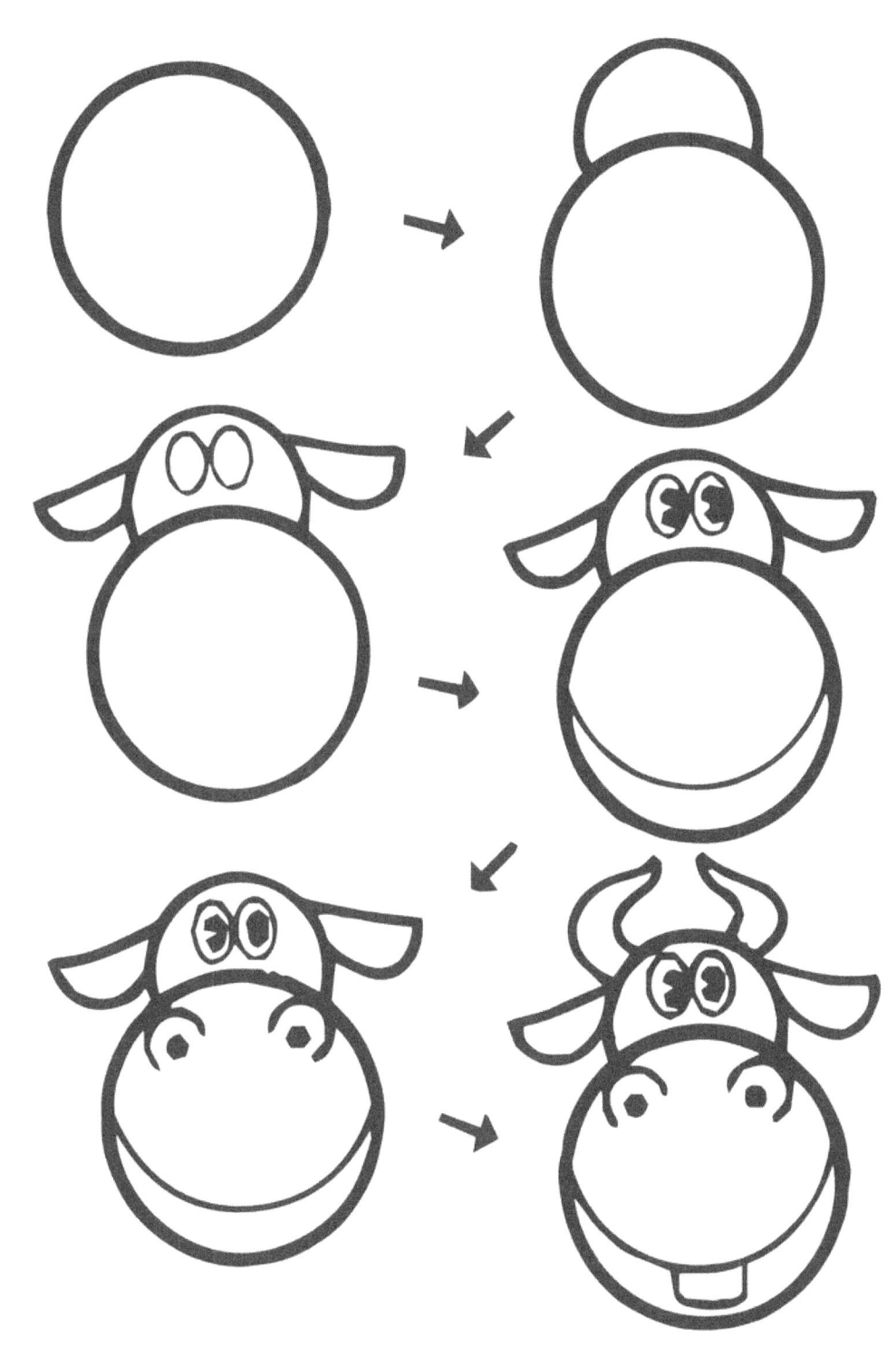

Draw Yourself

HOW TO DRAW CAT

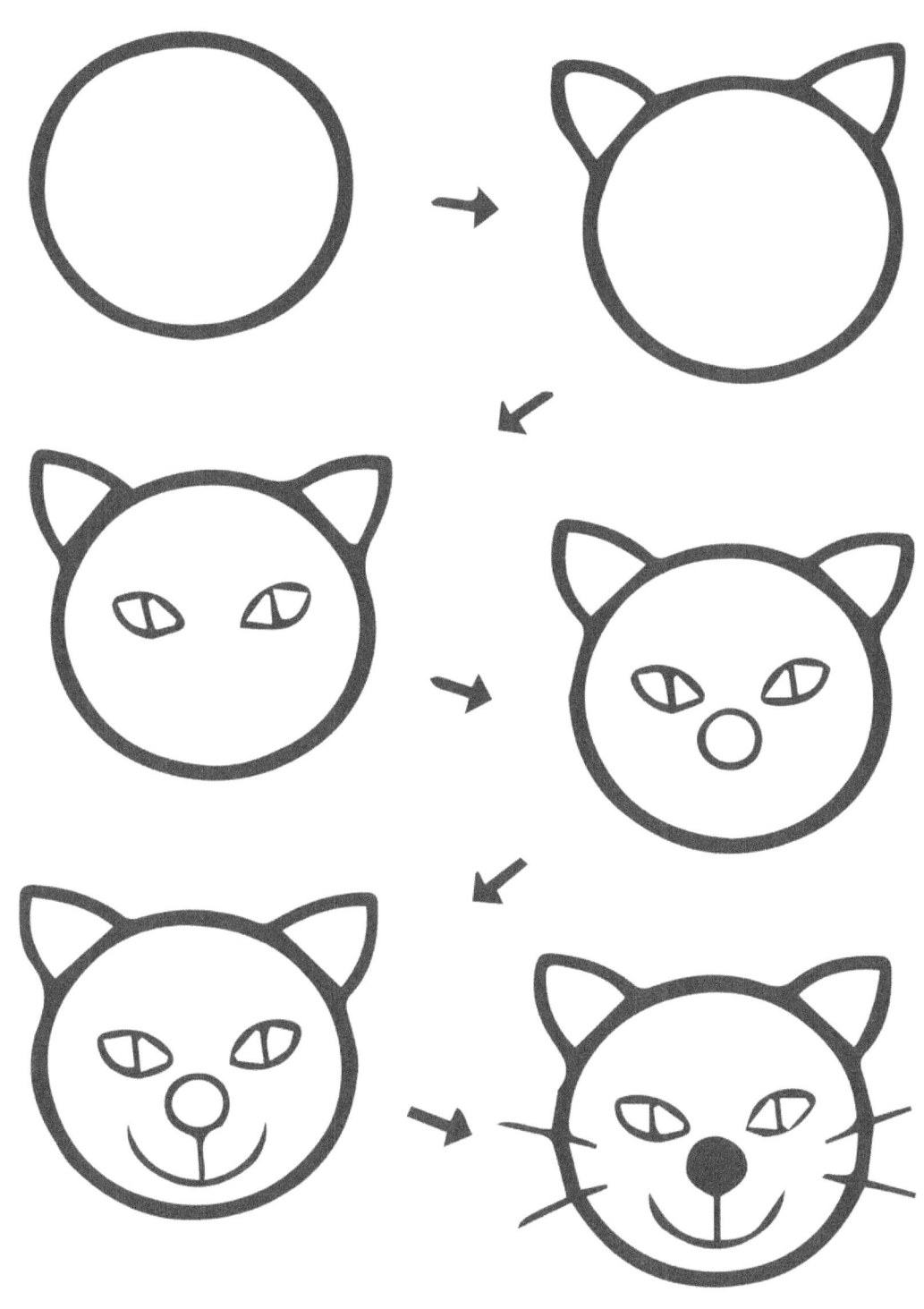

Draw Yourself

HOW TO DRAW CHICKEN

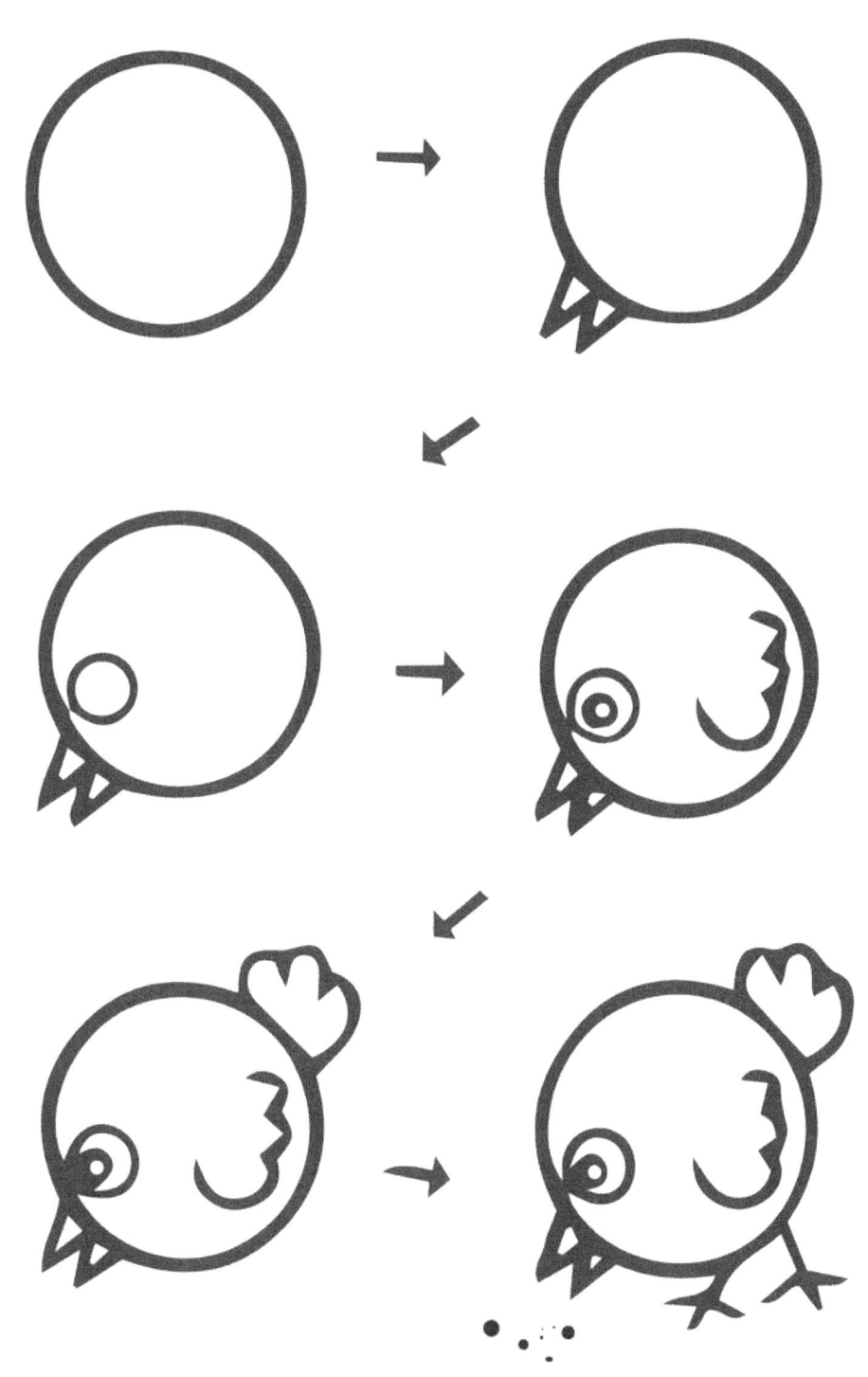

Draw Yourself

HOW TO DRAW CRAB

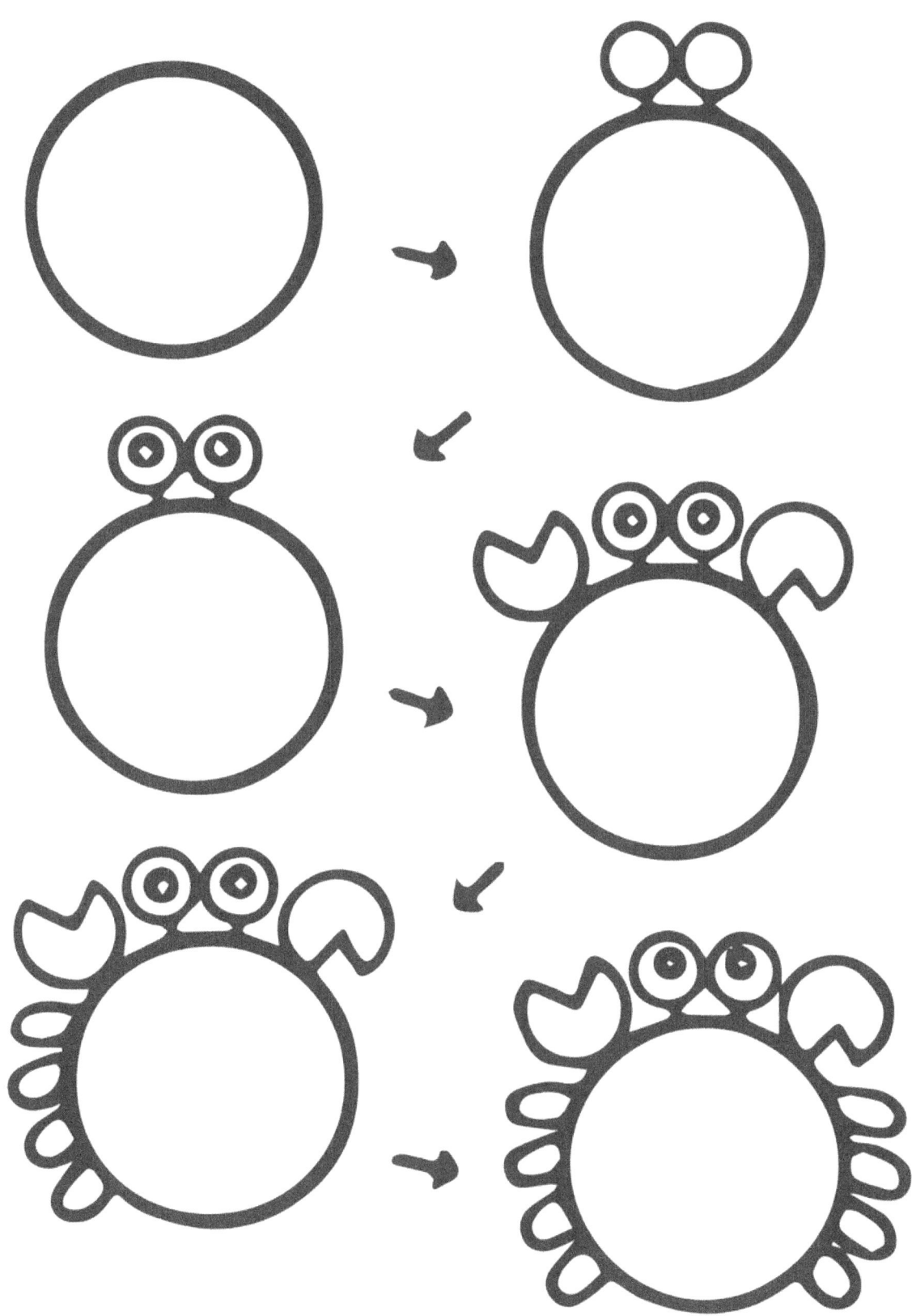

Draw Yourself

HOW TO DRAW DOG

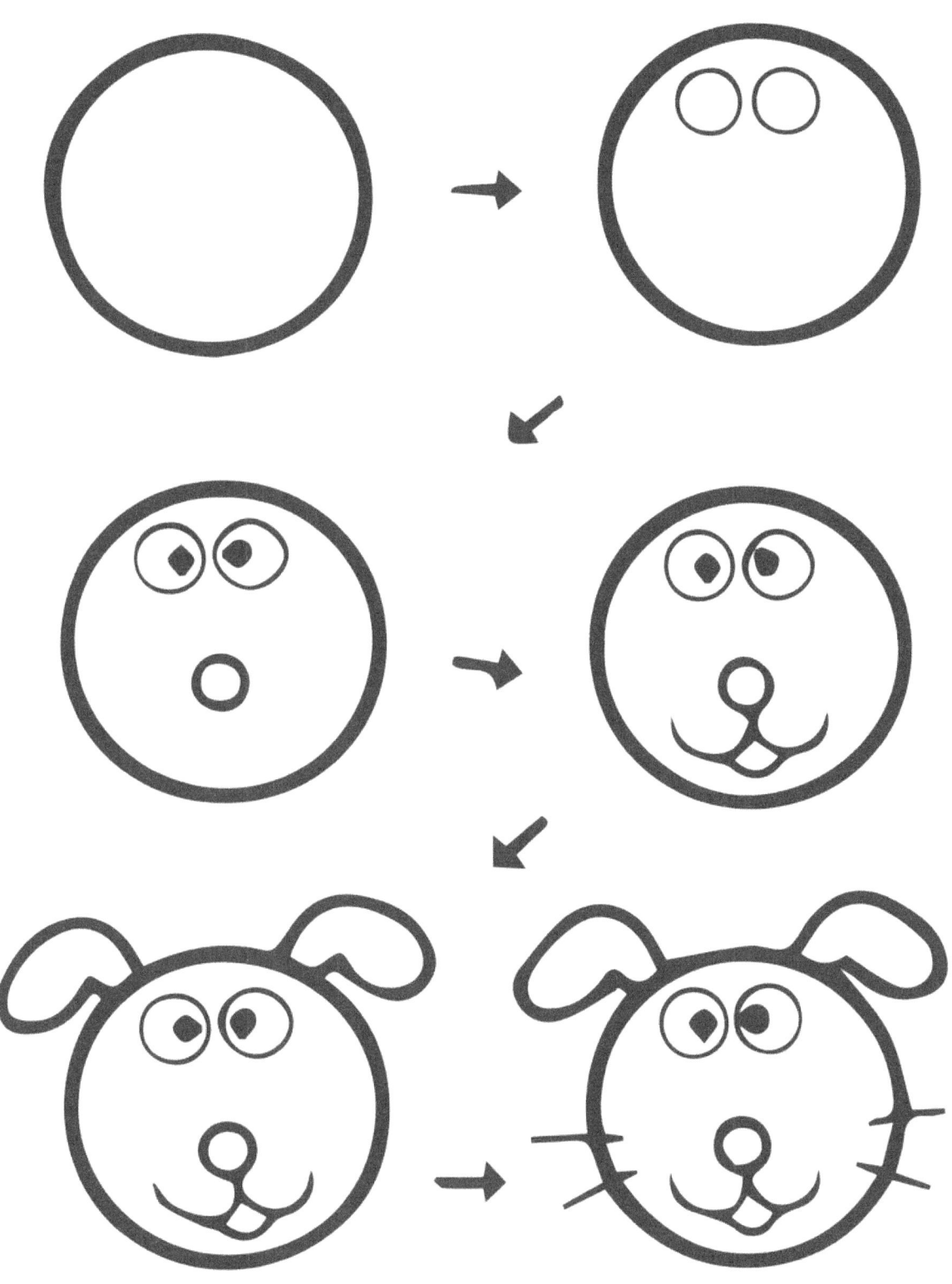

Draw Yourself

HOW TO DRAW EAGLE

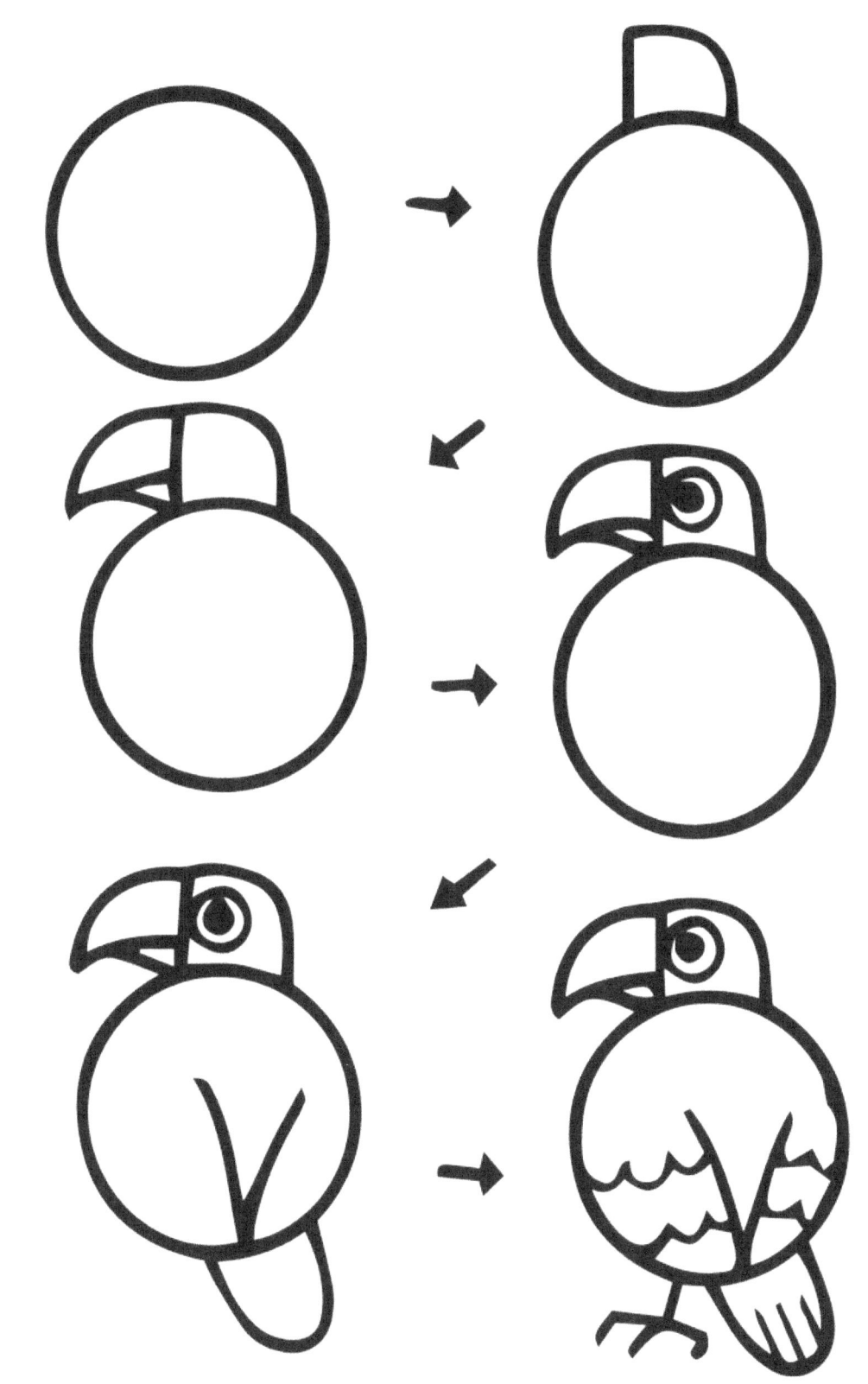

Draw Yourself

HOW TO DRAW FISH

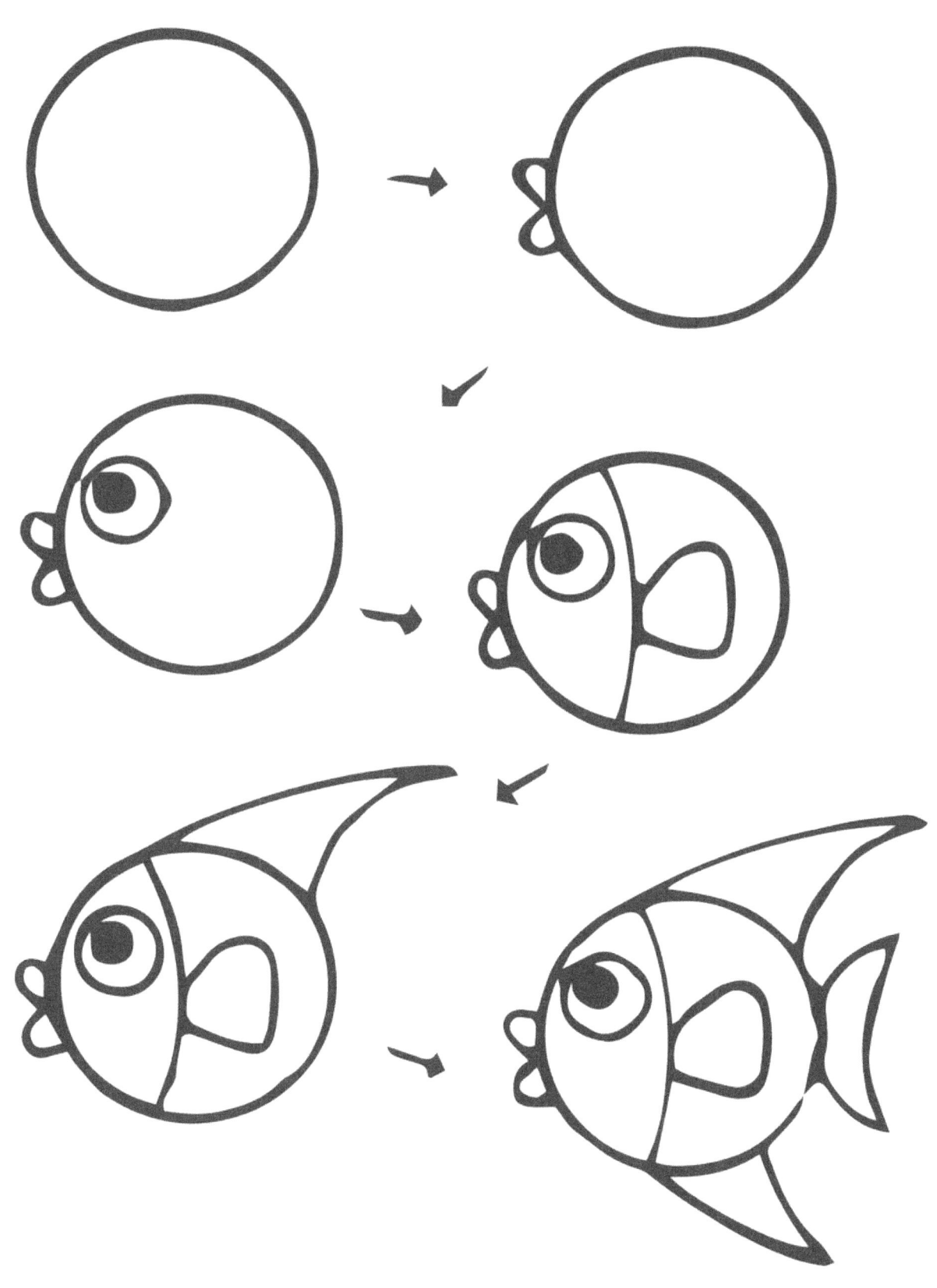

Draw Yourself

HOW TO DRAW GOLDFISH

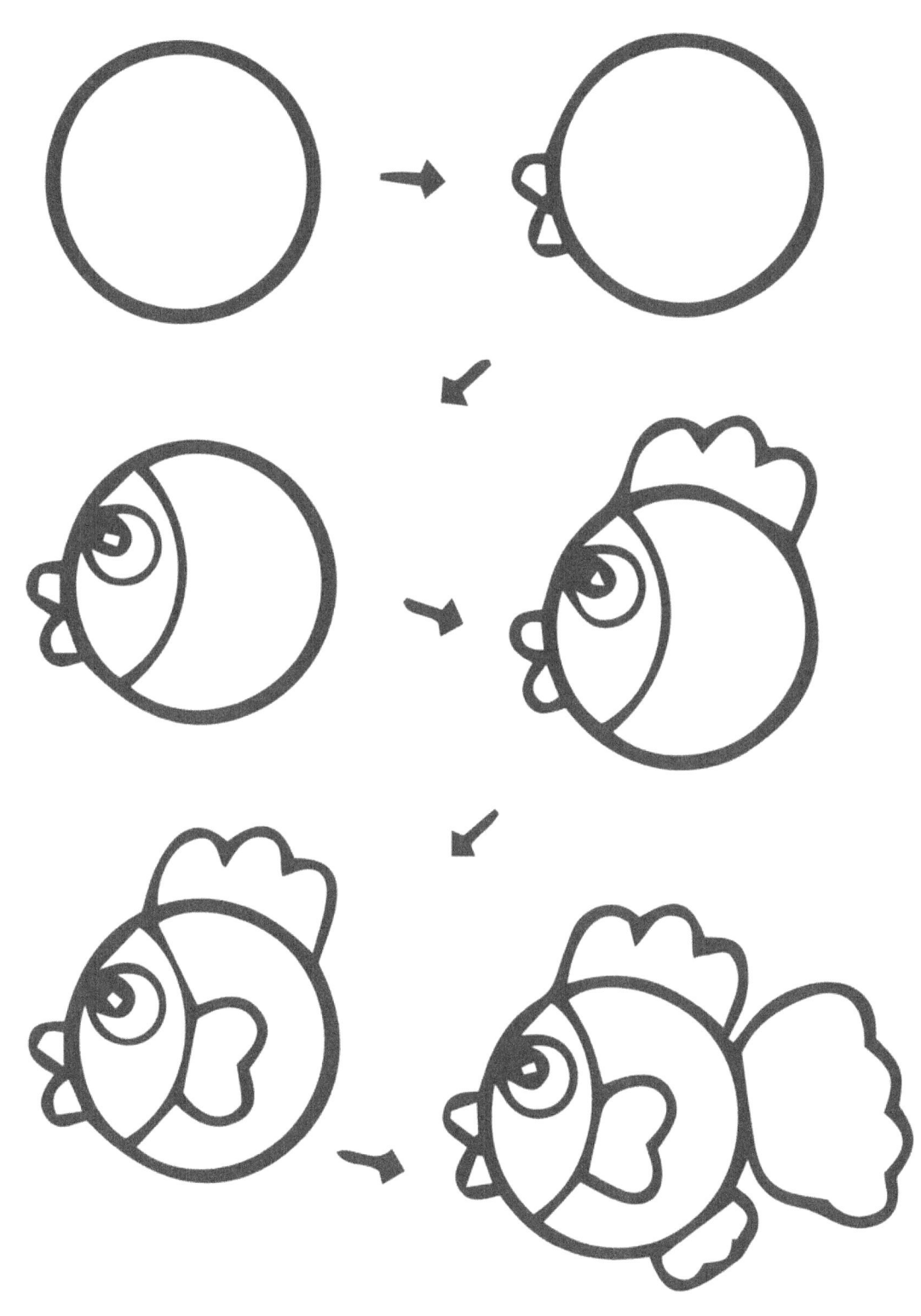

Draw Yourself

HOW TO DRAW HEN

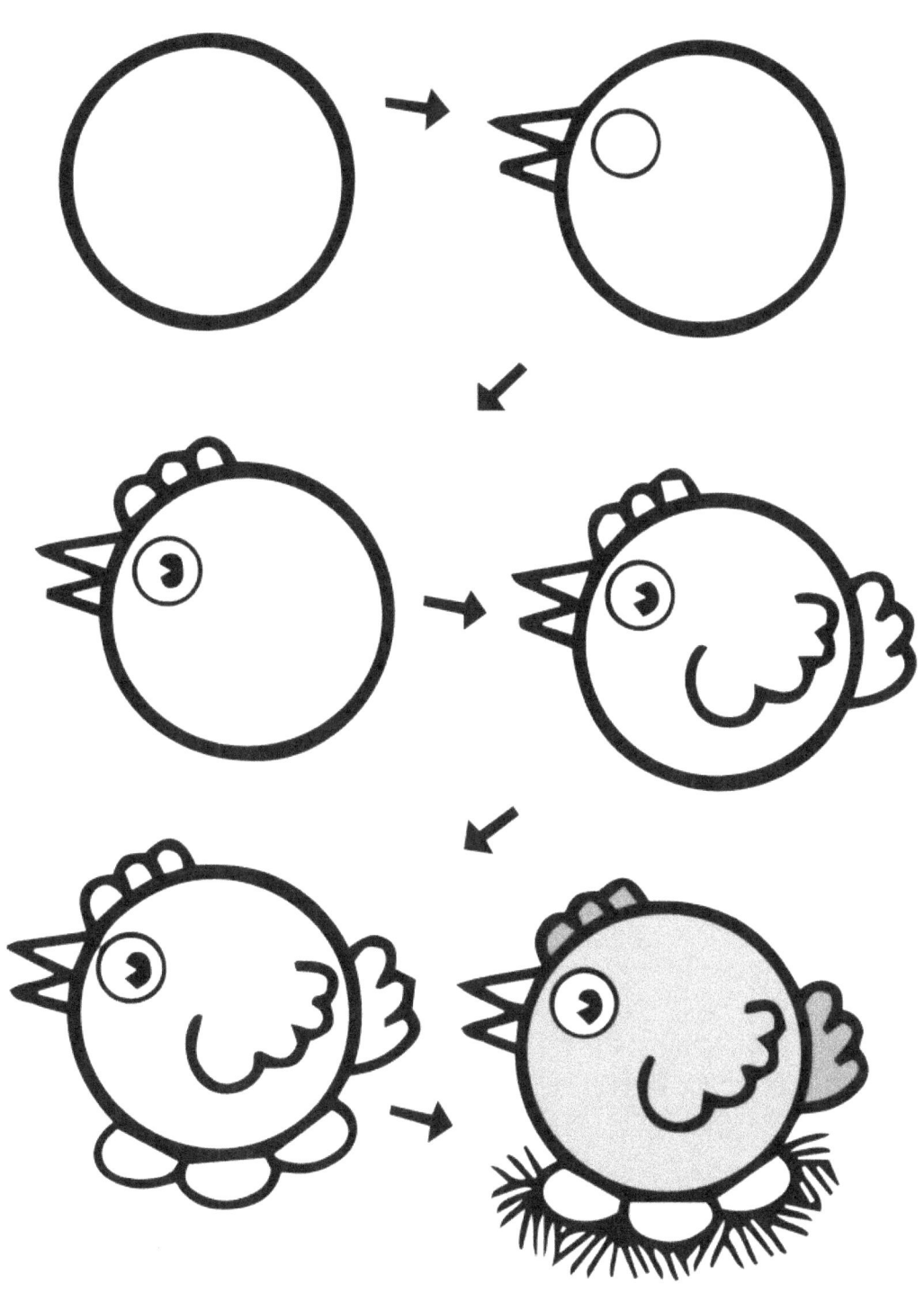

Draw Yourself

HOW TO DRAW LADYBUG

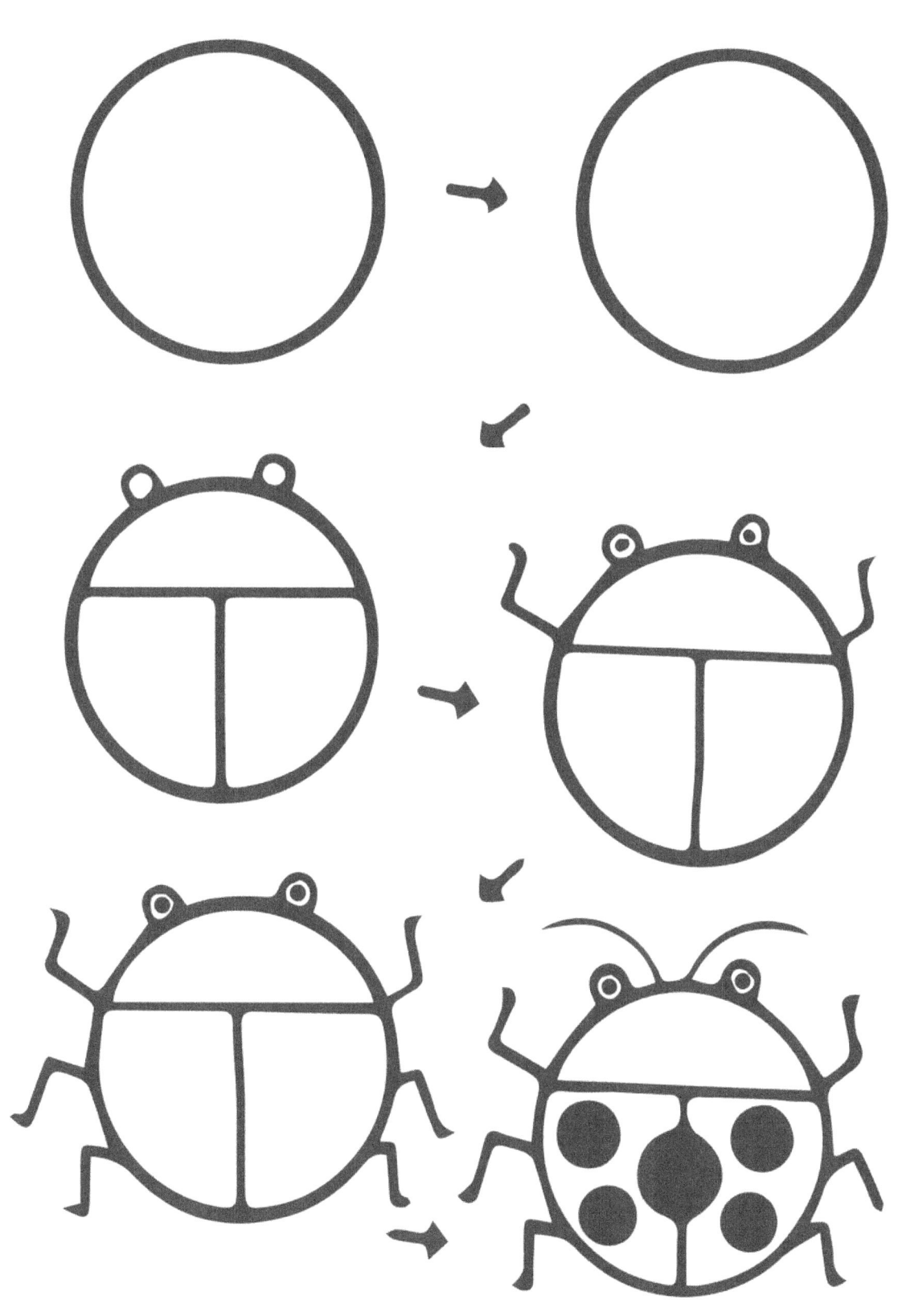

Draw Yourself

HOW TO DRAW MONKEY

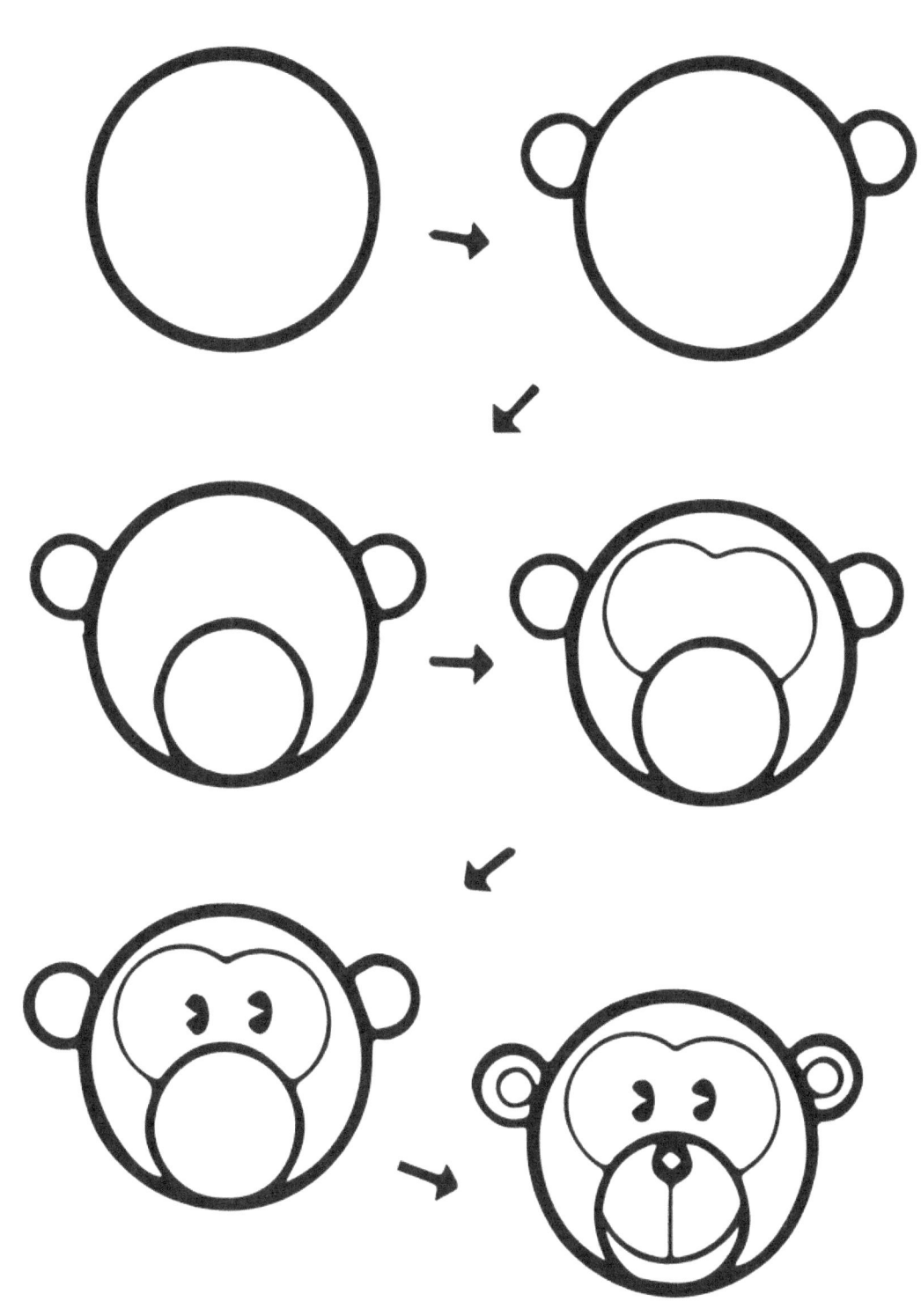

Draw Yourself

HOW TO DRAW NATIVE

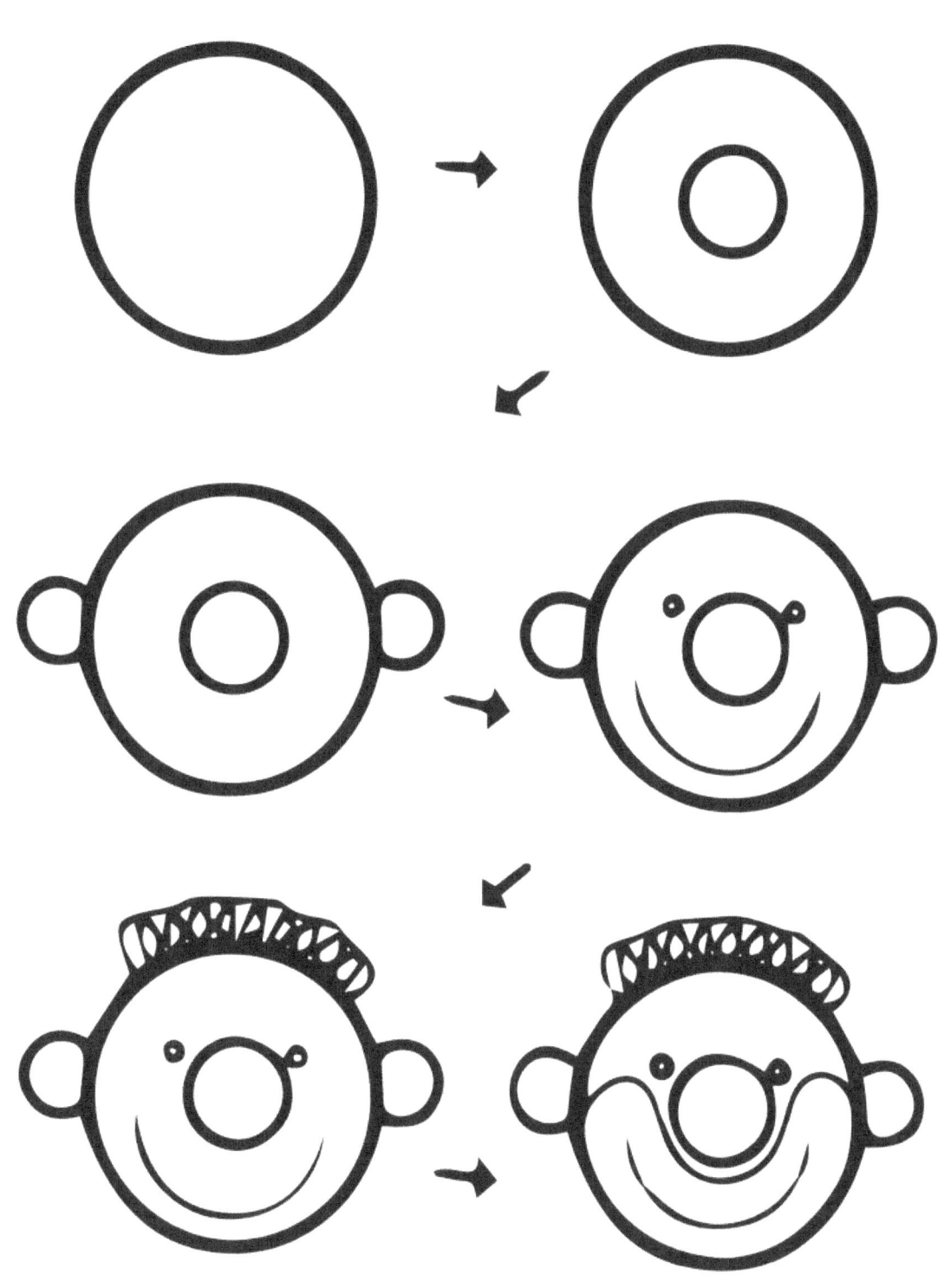

Draw Yourself

HOW TO DRAW OWL

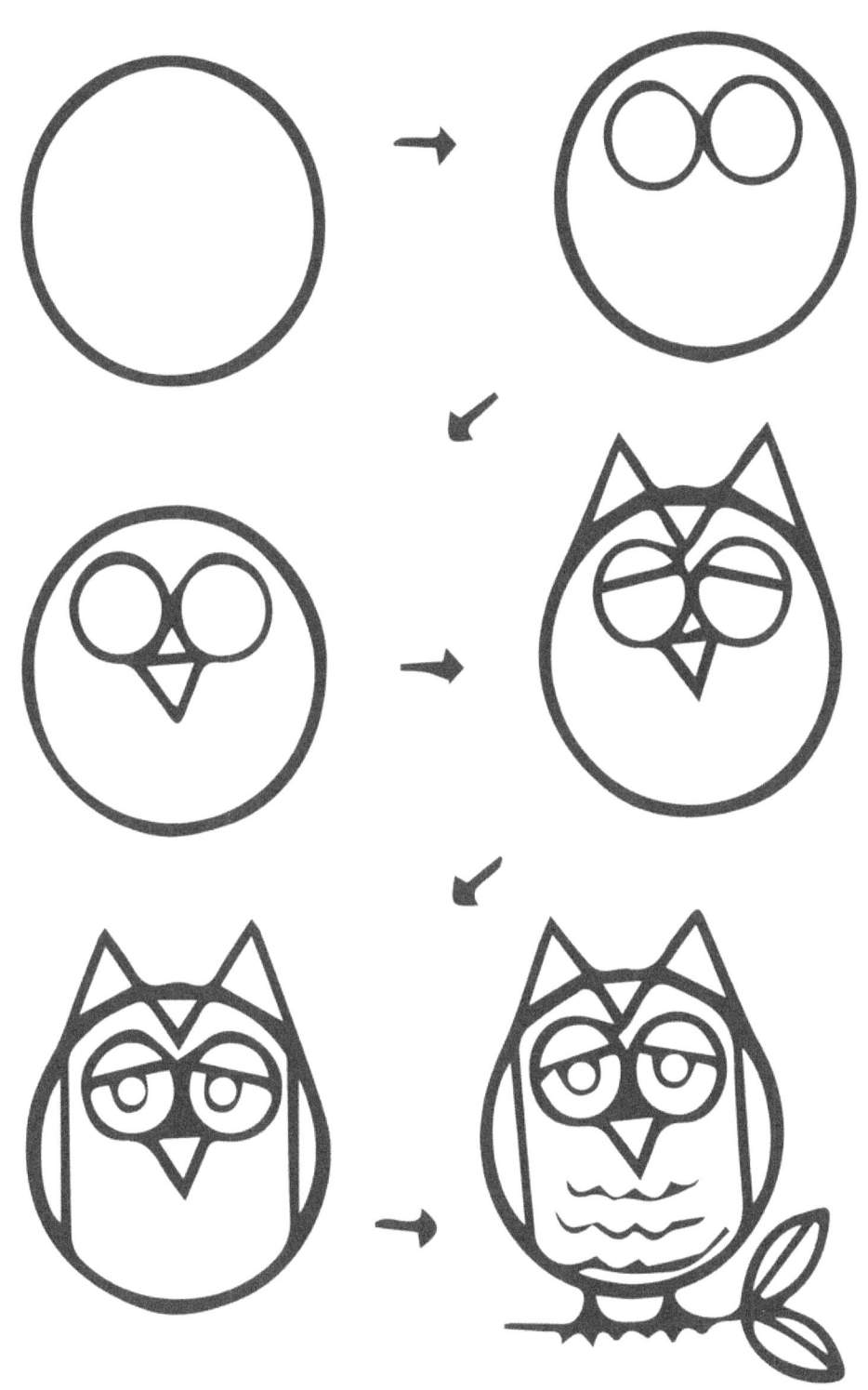

Draw Yourself

HOW TO DRAW OWL

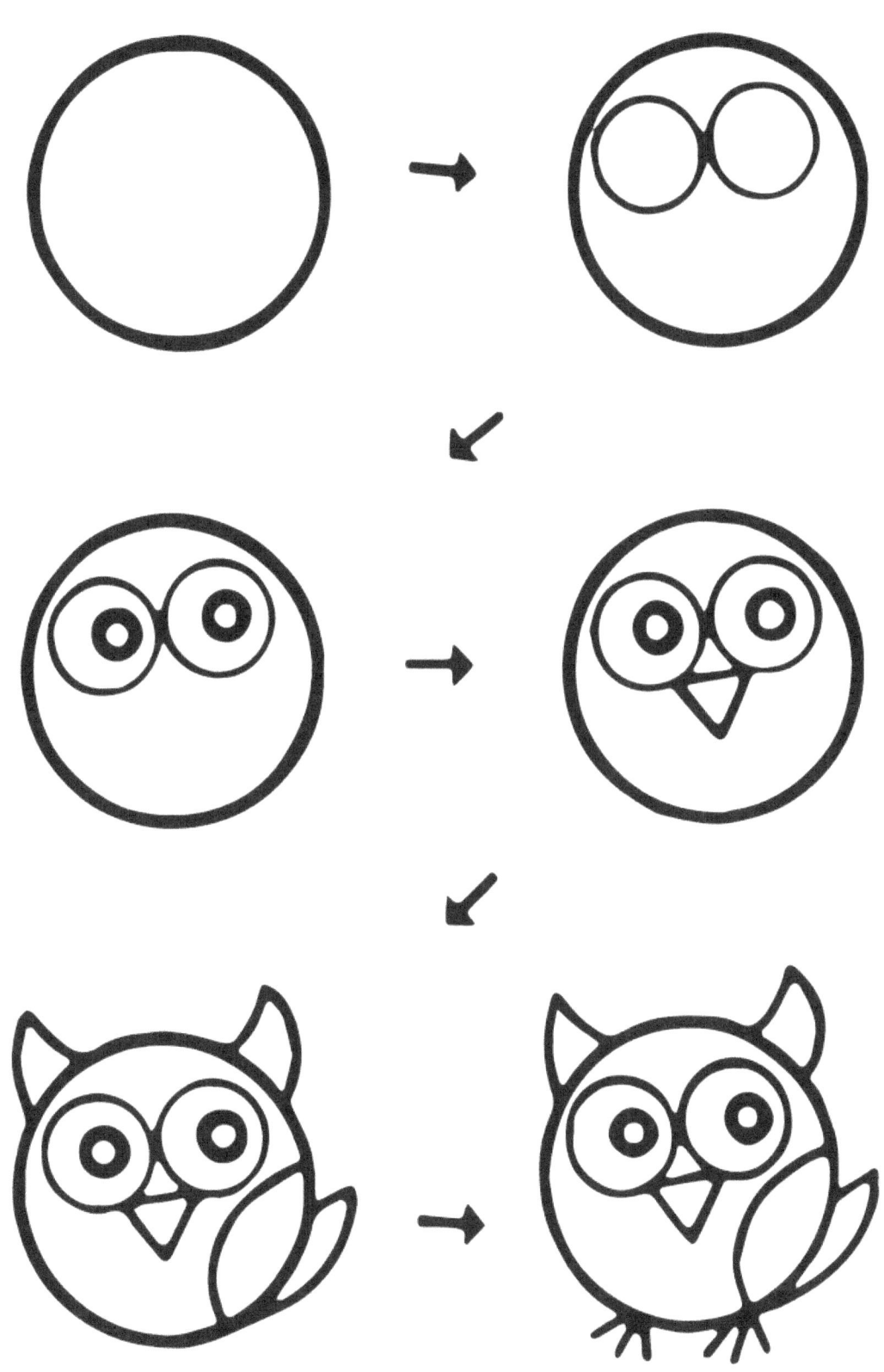

Draw Yourself

HOW TO DRAW PANDA

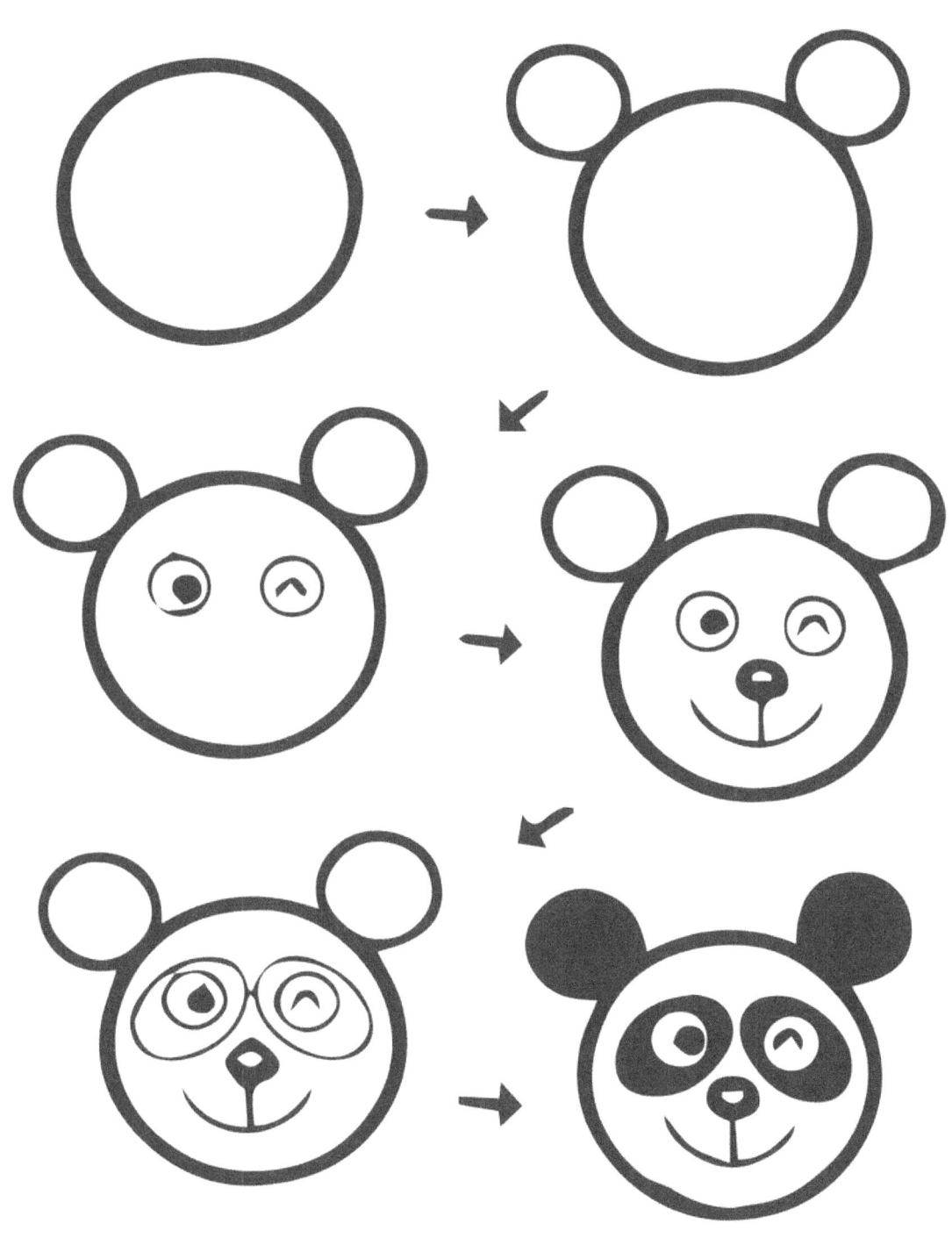

Draw Yourself

HOW TO DRAW RABBIT

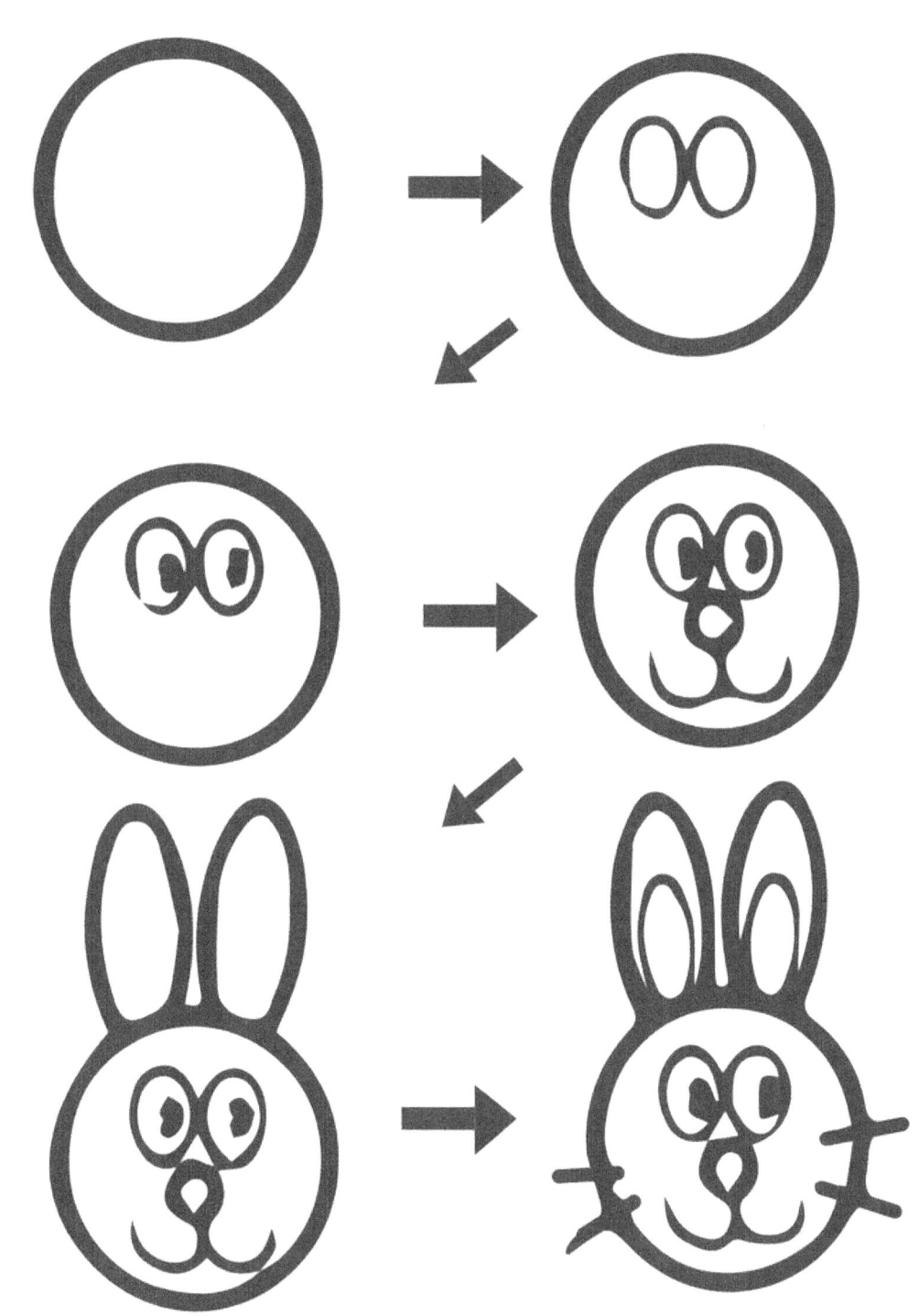

Draw Yourself

HOW TO DRAW ROOSTER

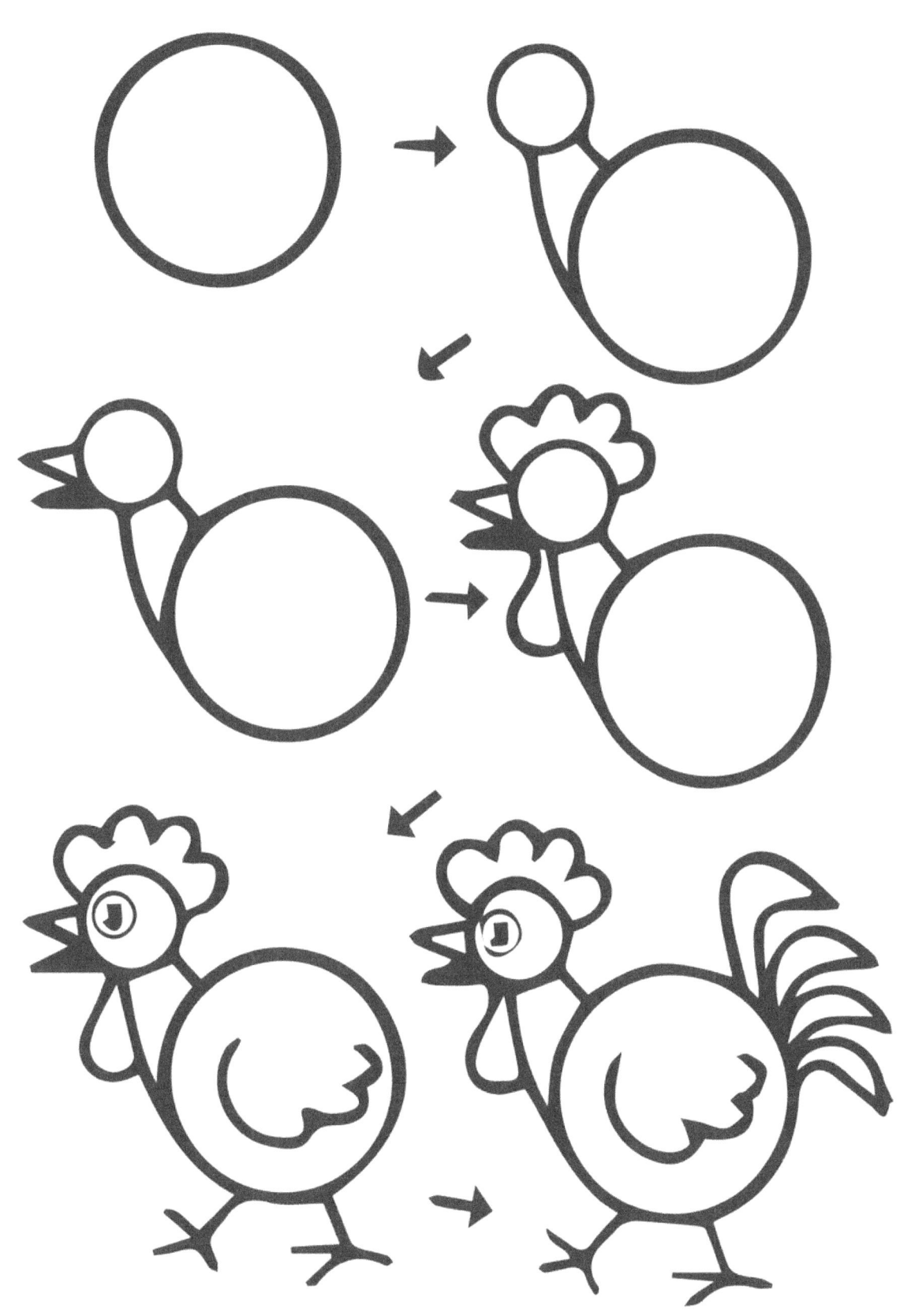

Draw Yourself

HOW TO DRAW SNAIL

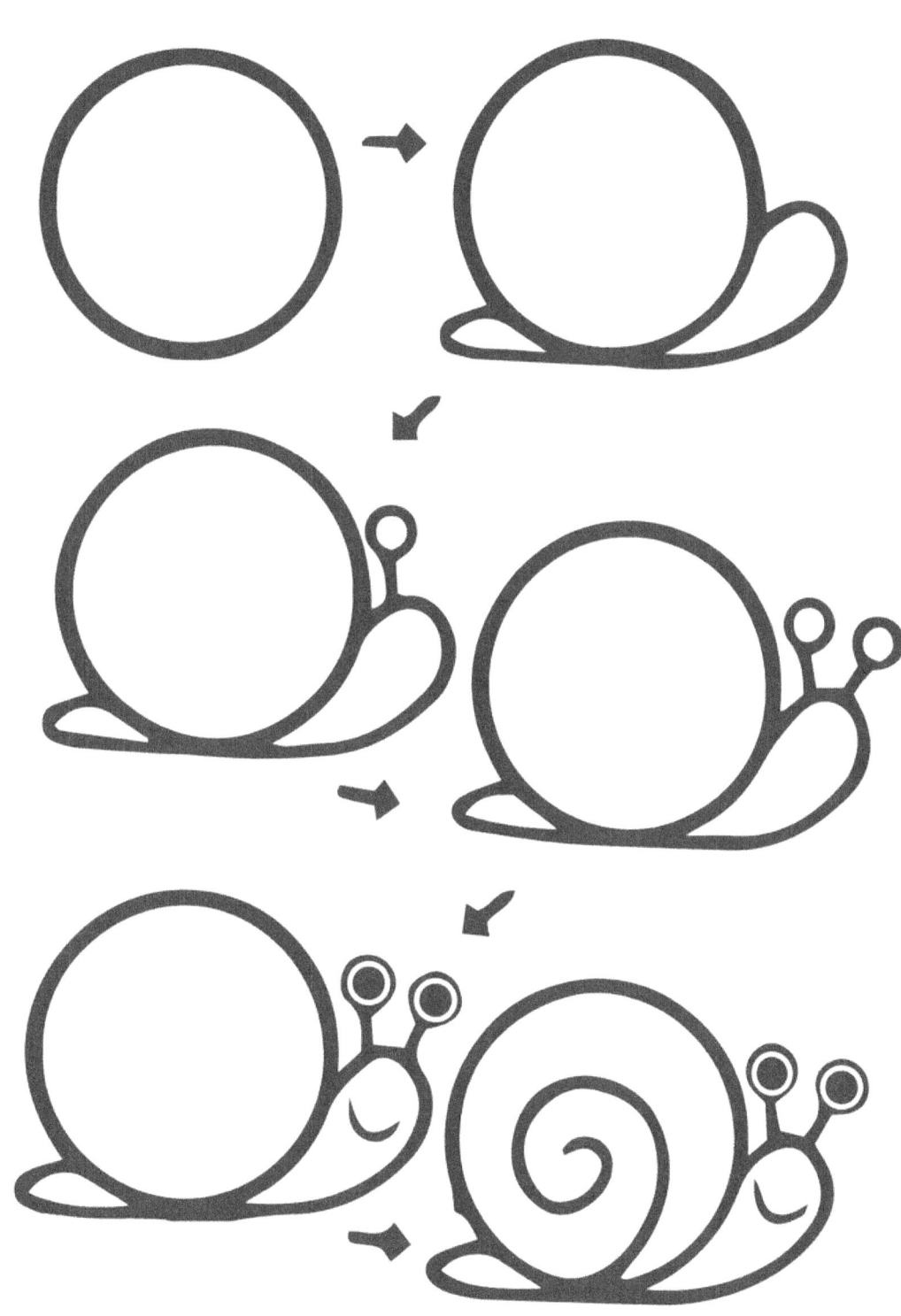

Draw Yourself

HOW TO DRAW SNAIL

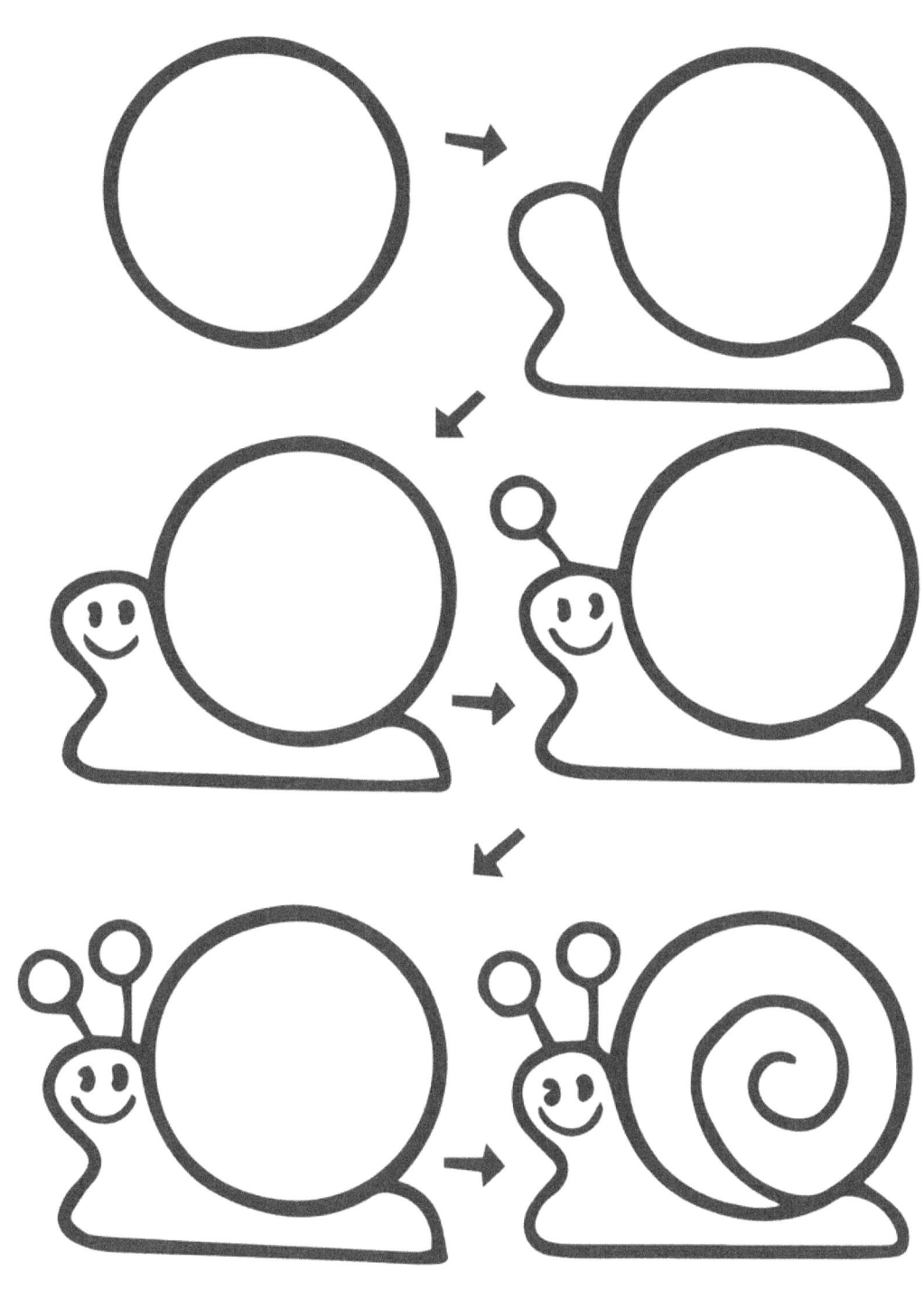

Draw Yourself

HOW TO DRAW SOLDIER

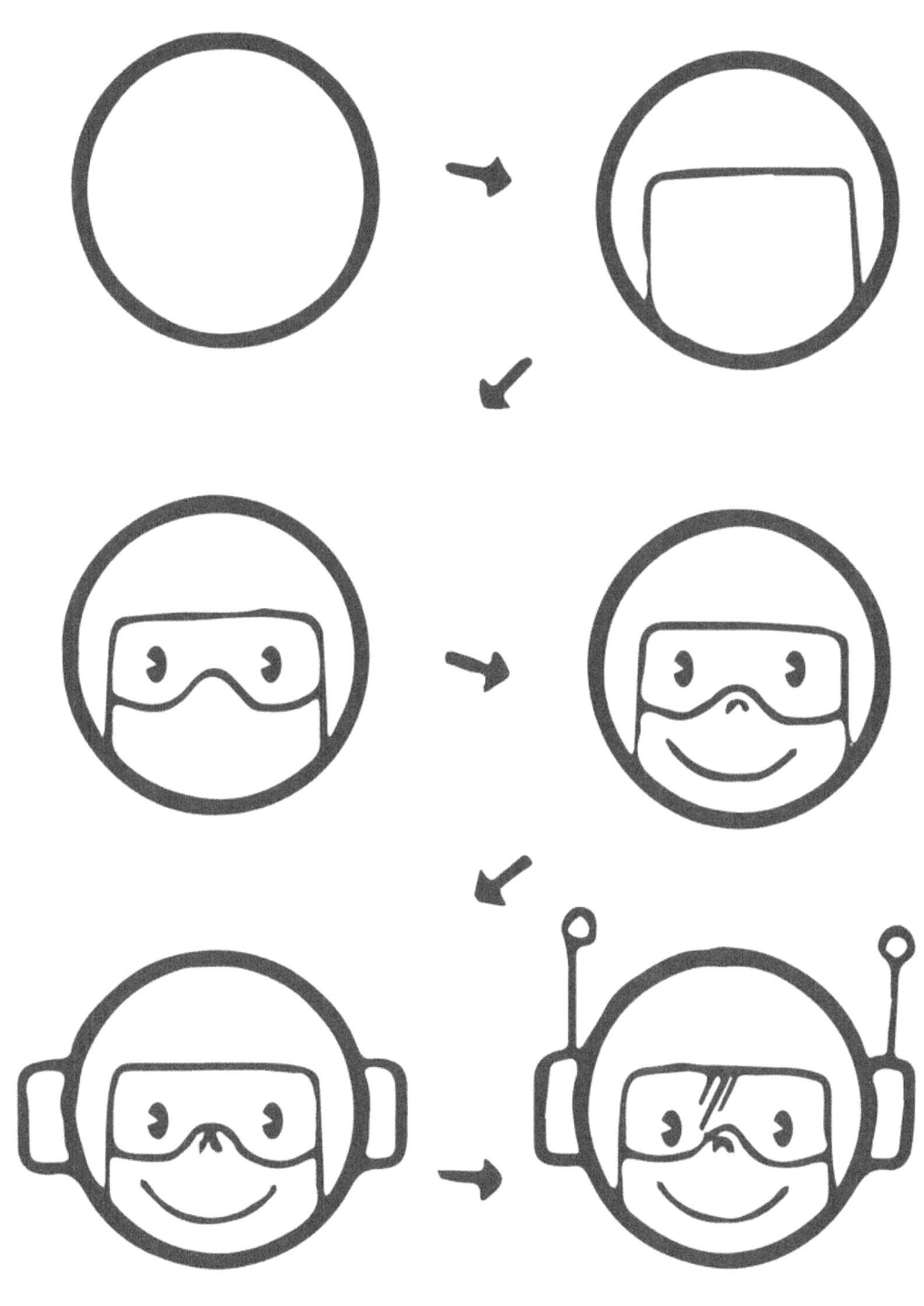

Draw Yourself

HOW TO DRAW SQUIRREL

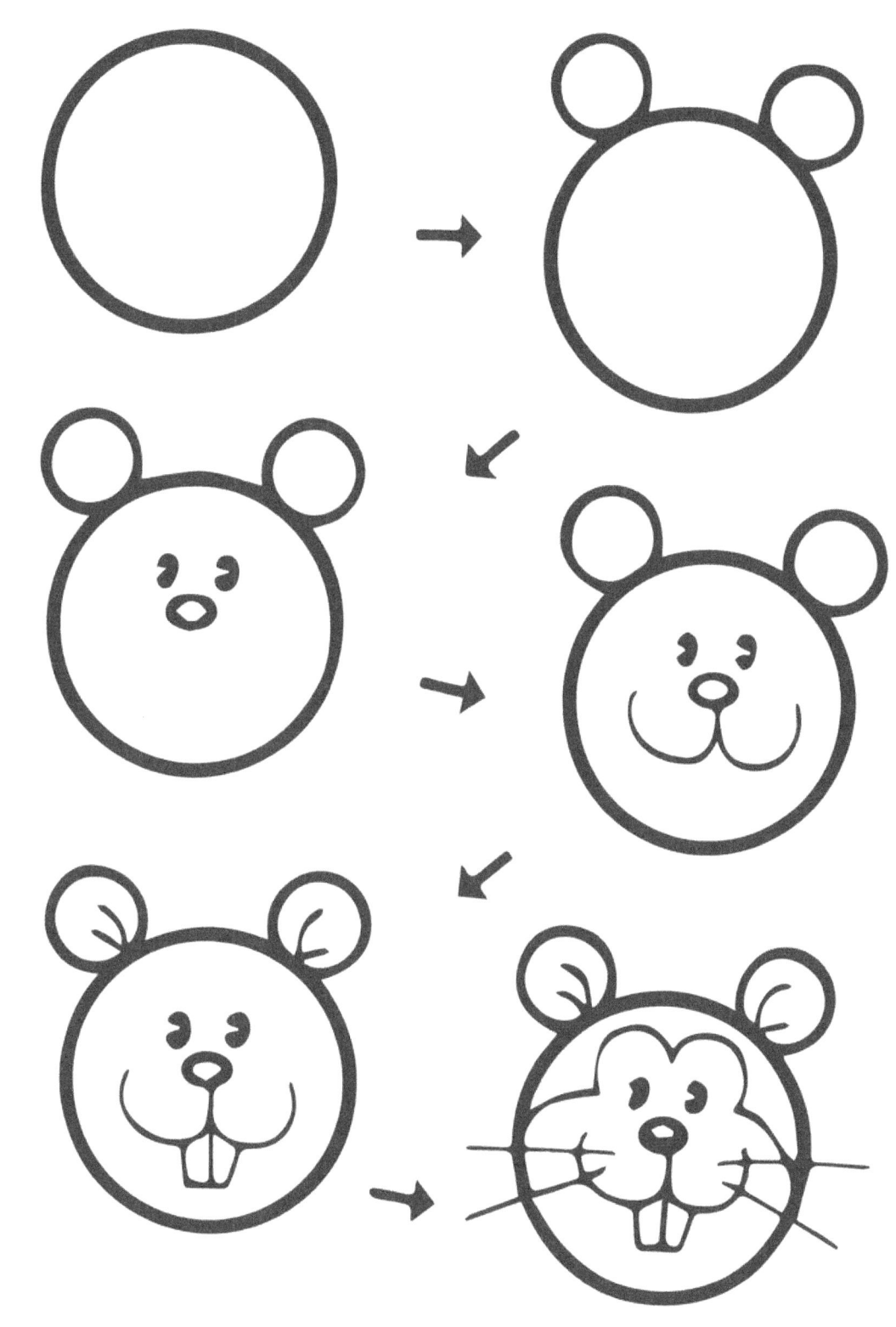

Draw Yourself

HOW TO DRAW SUN

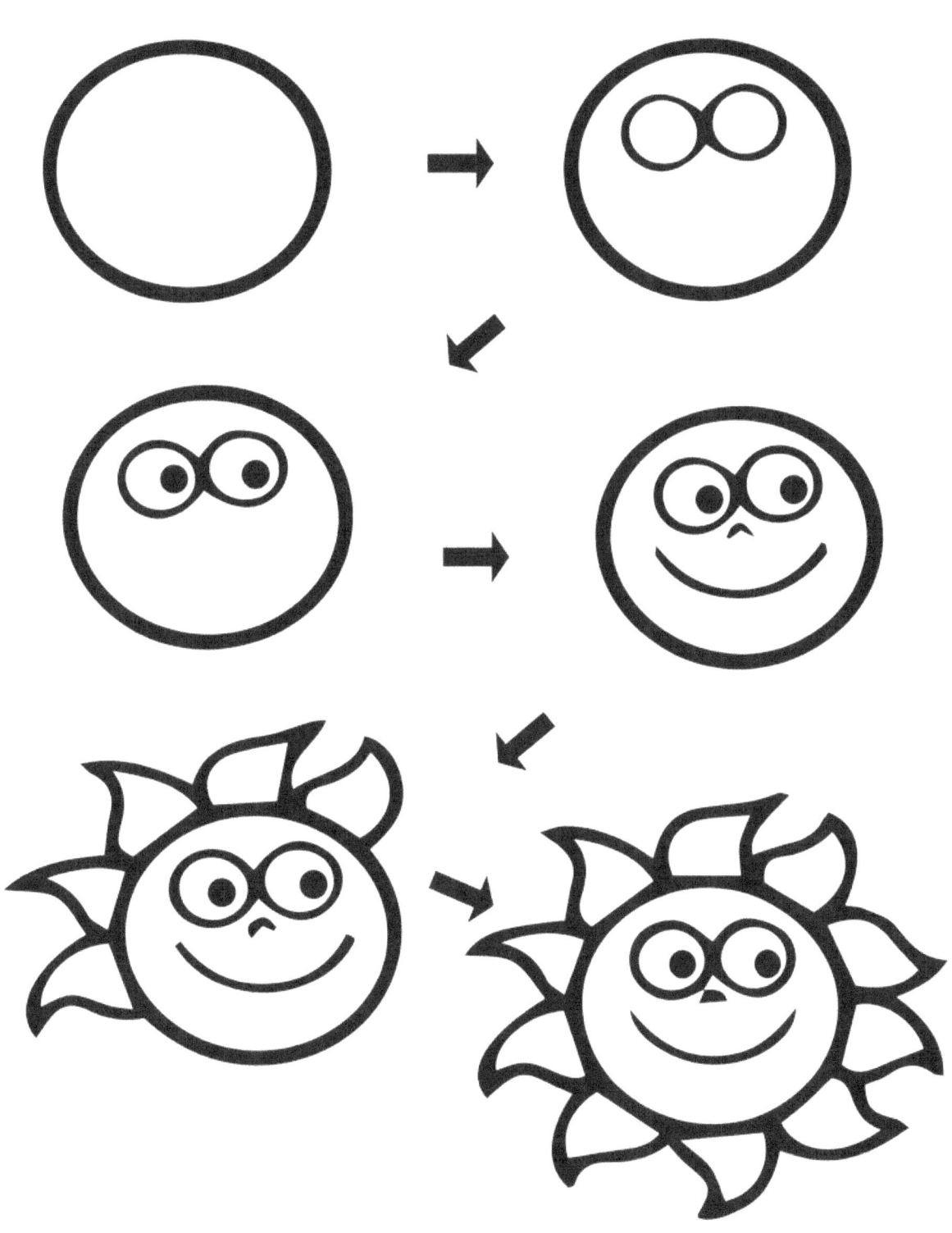

Draw Yourself

HOW TO DRAW TURKEY

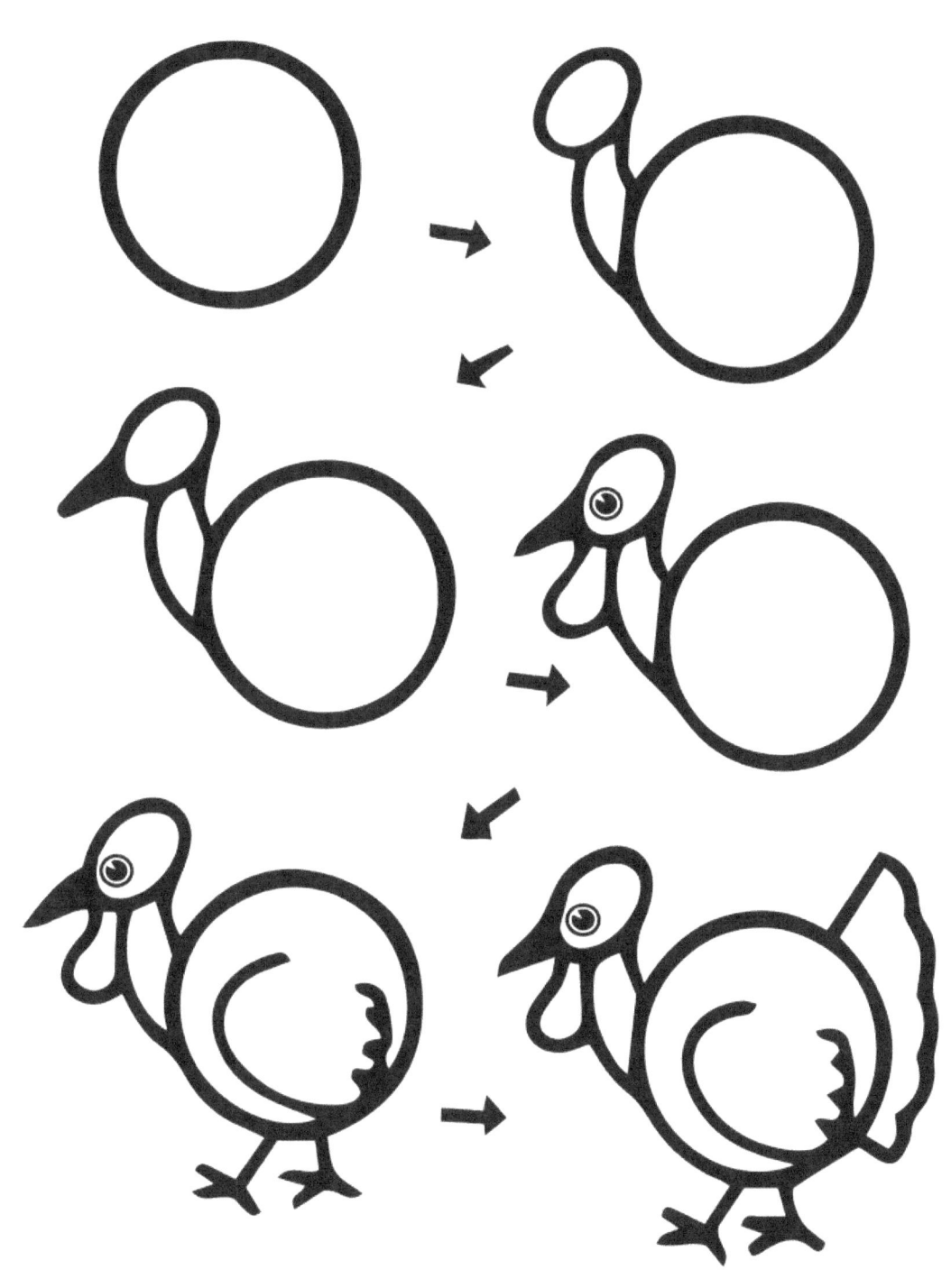

Draw Yourself

HOW TO DRAW TURTLE

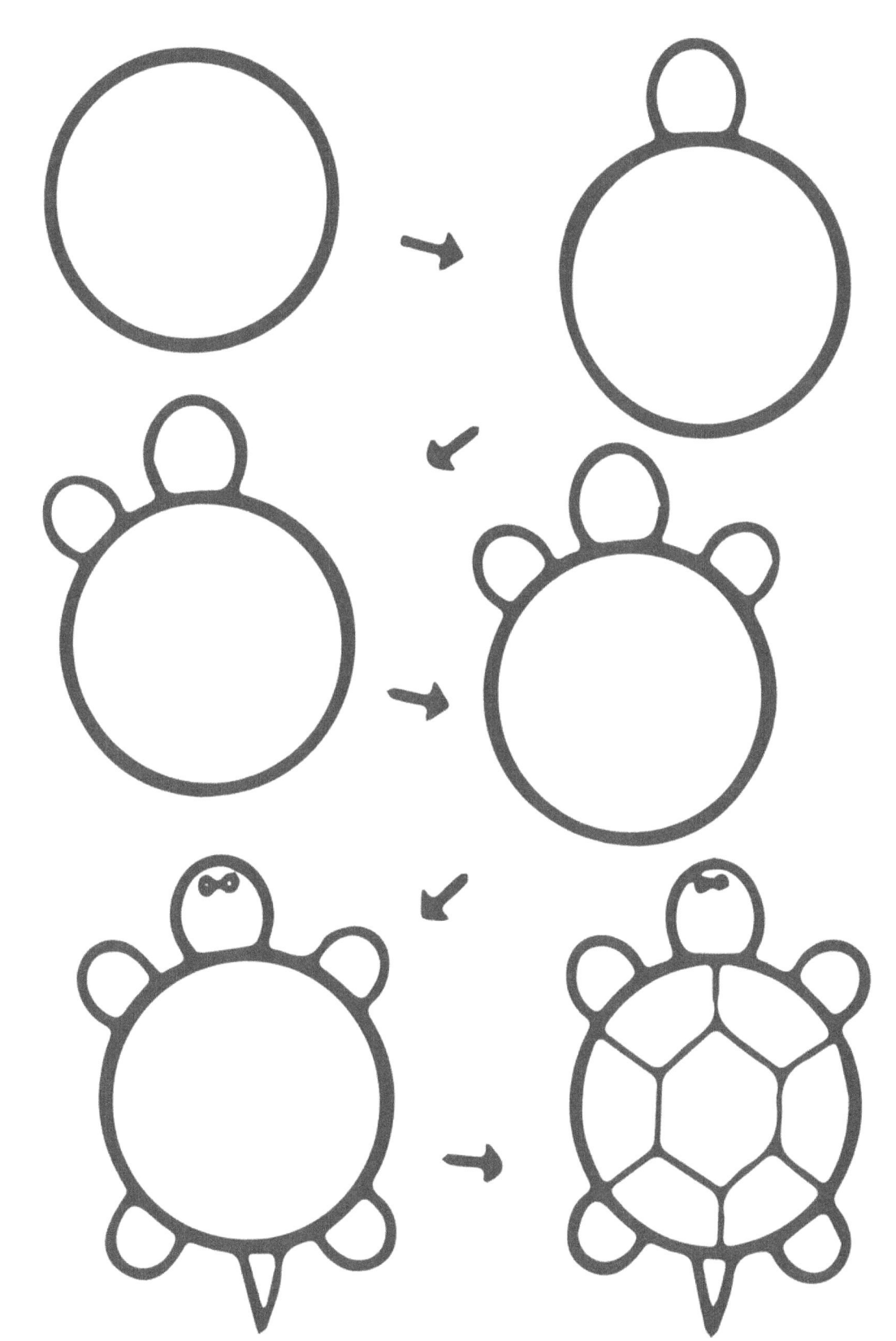